LOVE MOSAIC

MANY DIMENSIONS OF LOVE

HARINI V KUMAR

ISBN
Hardcase 979-8-89699-957-7
Paperback 979-8-89673-343-0

Editor: Aishwariya Kathiravan

Dedication

To my Mom,
My entire universe,

To my brother,
my unwavering strong suit,

To my family,
who may be unaware of my hidden verses,
yet have always filled my life with love.

And to my son,
my greatest muse,
May you uncover your own stories and never stop dreaming.

Foreword

Love is a force that defies easy definition, a kaleidoscope of emotions, connections, and transformations. Harini's collection of evocative poetry is a testament to love's boundless variations—its ability to surprise, to challenge, and to heal.

In these pages, you will find poems that explore love in all its myriad forms: the ecstatic highs of new romance, the quiet strength of enduring partnership, the bittersweet pangs of unrequited affection, and the profound bonds of friendship and family. These verses also delve into self-love, yearning born of desire, and the aching beauty of loss. For love, in all its iterations, shapes us in ways both subtle and profound.

Harini's words invite us to pause, reflect, and connect— to see ourselves and our relationships through fresh eyes. They remind us that love is as much about giving as it is about receiving, as much about courage as it is about vulnerability.

As you journey through this collection, allow yourself to feel the weight and wonder of each poem. Let the words resonate, stir memories, and ignite new realisations. May this book serve as a gentle companion in your exploration of love, offering glimpses of its essence and reflections of your own heart.

Ayesha Inoon
Author of Untethered / Winner of the 2022 ASA/
HQ Fiction Prize.

* * *

Bessy Reads

First, a big thank you!

On behalf of Bessy Reads, it is an absolute honor to introduce *Love Mosaic*, a beautifully evocative debut by Harini. At its heart, this book is a celebration of the many dimensions of love—a timeless force that shapes us, binds us, and illuminates our humanity. Through her poignant reflections and tender prose, Harini invites us into a world where love unfolds in its myriad forms: familial, romantic, selfless, and introspective.

As a community that thrives on stories and shared connections, Bessy Reads is inspired by Harini's ability to transform everyday moments into profound narratives. Her words remind us that love is not confined to grand gestures or fleeting romances—it is present in the silence of a mother's embrace, the laughter shared between friends, and the quiet resilience of the human spirit.

This collection is more than just a book; it is an invitation to pause, reflect, and connect with the emotions that make us beautifully human. Whether you are a seasoned reader or new to the world of poetry and personal essays, *Love Mosaic* promises to resonate with your heart and offer solace, joy, and a sense of shared belonging.

As you turn these pages, may you find fragments of your own story woven into Harini's words, and may her reflections spark moments of introspection and connection in your journey.

Welcome to the world of *Love Mosaic*.

With love and light,

Bessy Reads

* * *

Like a breeze on the evening, Harini's Love Mosaic caresses her readers. The poems are fresh, aesthetic, clear and simple in language that even first time poem readers in english can engulf it's essence easily. There are variety of topics to exlpore like romance, infactuation, spiritual love relishing different kinds of taste. Such a beautifully crafted book holding a feast for its readers. All the best to Harini on her gracious poem book !

Revanthi Aazhisai
Author of Kaarkala Anangu

About the Book

In a world filled with connections, love remains one of the most profound experiences that we share as human beings.

This book invites readers to embark on one such experience that explores the many dimensions of love, revealing its complexities and nuances.

It reflects on the moments that bring us closer to one another and the feelings that challenge our hearts. Through very mundane narratives and insightful thoughts, may we delve deep into the bonds that evoke joy, heartache and everything in between.

This journey speaks love in all its manifestations, not just as a feeling, but the very essence of what it means to be human, reminding us of our shared stories and the beauty of vulnerability.

A Letter to My Readers

Dear Beloved Readers,

As I sit down to write this letter, my heart is filled with a mix of excitement and uncertainty. You are about to onboard a journey that is very close to my heart—my debut book, a collection born from countless scribbled notes and moments of reflection on love lost and the weight of longing.

This book is a piece of my soul, an exploration of emotions that many of us share but often find difficult to express. Each page draws from my own experiences and the universal threads that I believe to connect us all, the warmth of love that once was, the heartache of goodbyes and the lingering echoes of what could have been. My hope is that you will find a reflection of your own experiences between these pages, resonating with both the beauty and pain that love can bring.

Writing this book has been both a healing process and a celebration—a way to honour the beauty of relationships and its complexity in every form of love, while I have also enjoyed throwing in some random scribbles of my own interest for fiction in a humorous way to lighten up the mood.

Thank you for allowing me to share this intimate piece of myself with you. I hope it reverberates with you, offering solace in moments of solitude and sparks of hope amidst heartache. Remember, we are all navigating the life of love together, and in this shared experience, we find strength. May this book offer you comfort, introspection and perhaps even the reassurance that you are not alone in your own explorations.

Contents

Spiritual Love

Love for Humanity

Familial Love

Companionship

Contents

Treasured Memories

Love for Foods

Friendship

Spiritual Love

Sacred Presence

In the quiet moments of dawn,
when the world is still, I feel the gentle whisper,
calling out to me. The sun,
which rises like a promise, everyday, reminding me that I am
part of a greater design. In each breath, I find a reflection, a
sacred rhythm that binds my spirit to the infinite.

As I gaze into the starry sky, I sense the thread that
connects me to this earth, it is in these sacred spaces,
that I recognize the divine reflection within and the unity of
all beings.
I am reminded that I am never alone.
I am part of something,
beautifully,
vast.

Ties with My Soul

In the silence of the night, the waves intertwine,
like shadows dancing beneath the moon's gentle glow. Each
drop of water is a prayer, a reminder of all that exists, flowing
effortlessly towards the shore.

In this sacred dance between land and sea, I acknowledge the
higher power that embodies love, guiding me toward
my true self.
Shadows dance and even when they flicker,
I see a guiding light, steady,
leading me to my soul.
This unseen presence cradles me like a
mother's embrace,
reminding me of my worth, my purpose.

Through trials that test my spirit, I am not alone, this power,
fortifies my resolve. When I wander through life's darkest maze,
this higher power nudges me to the light. It is here that
I discover my authentic voice, no longer shackled by
doubt or despair.
The universe conspires in my favor, revealing the beauty of
becoming your true self and in its embrace,
I find home.

Love for Humanity

Sanctuary

Beneath the surface of every smile, lies an untold story,
waiting for a kind heart to listen and understand. Like a
lighthouse
on a stormy night, compassion shines brightly, offering peace
to weary soul lost in the chaos of life.

In the act of listening, we unfold layers of pain and joy,
reverberating with the essence of our shared consciousness.
When we practice empathy, we weave together a quilt of
belongings
by providing warmth and shelter in times of need by creating
a safe space where humanity thrives.

Each sigh carries a hint of longing,
every tear, a proof of struggle
felt by countless others.

When we engage in their conversation,
it heals them and sometimes us,
while we reveal different dimensions of sorrow and happiness,
echoing the core of our humanity,
a profound connection begins
and selflessness becomes second nature, enriching
both giver and receiver.

Rich Tapestry

Compassion is the quiet call that stirs us from smugness,
beckoning us to reach out when the world feels heavy.

In a world filled with divisions,
empathy stands as our guiding star
by lighting pathways towards connection.

Each altruistic act becomes a ripple,
a gentle push that inspires others to join the dance.

Through the lens of love, our differences melt away,
revealing a rich tapestry woven from
countless smiles.

Familial Love

Forever Their Guardian

In the soft light of dawn, a mother cradles her sleeping child,
her heart composing an invisible form of love. Every gentle
breath shared is a promise,
every heartbeat, a testament to their new world
that knows no boundaries.

Each shared moment, a seed planted in rich soil, nourished
by kindness and unyielding support.
In her eyes, the child sees an unwavering love,
a light that will guide them through.

A father's rough hands hold his little ones,
lifting them above the Universe,
where worries fade and laughter reigns.
It matters not who wins or loses;
every moment shared is a treasure,
each smile a reminder of their bond.

Love, That Feels Cozy

Seated in a cozy armchair,
grandfather shares tales of his youth,
each word sounds the best as a bridge,
connecting generations.
The curious little eyes wide, the child leans closer,
as if he understood every word,
even though he is just an infant,
captivated by his grandfather's love pouring aura.

In a vibrant garden,
grandmother shows how to nurture the plants,
hands digging deep into the soil.
Each seed planted is a lesson in growth,
patience and resilience, mirrored in the love she sows.

Later that evening,
they gather with colored pencils and papers,
doodling dreams and wishes, which she never got to experience,
but longed for.
With each stoke of colorful realm,
they find joy in being themselves, knowing she too became a
kid once again.

Companionship

Silent Words

In the stillness of shared moments,
our closeness flourishes without words.
With each step, we gather stories like treasures,
rich with lessons and laughter.

In our companionship,
we share burdens, growing stronger
with each trial faced.

In every heartbeat,
we hear the promise of loyalty,
unwavering amidst life's chaos.
Our bond teaches us that strength
comes from togetherness.
Side by side, we create a mosaic
of shared experiences, bright and vivid.

In this companionship, we learn that love
knows no boundaries.

Together on the Playground

Playground is where we explore, laugh, and sometimes stumble together. Each encounter is a game we play, filled with joy and adventure. We leap over obstacles, inventing our own rules as we go.

In the sweetest moments, time seems to stand still, and our bond grows deeper. In this connection, we find a sense of belonging that fills our souls.

Romance

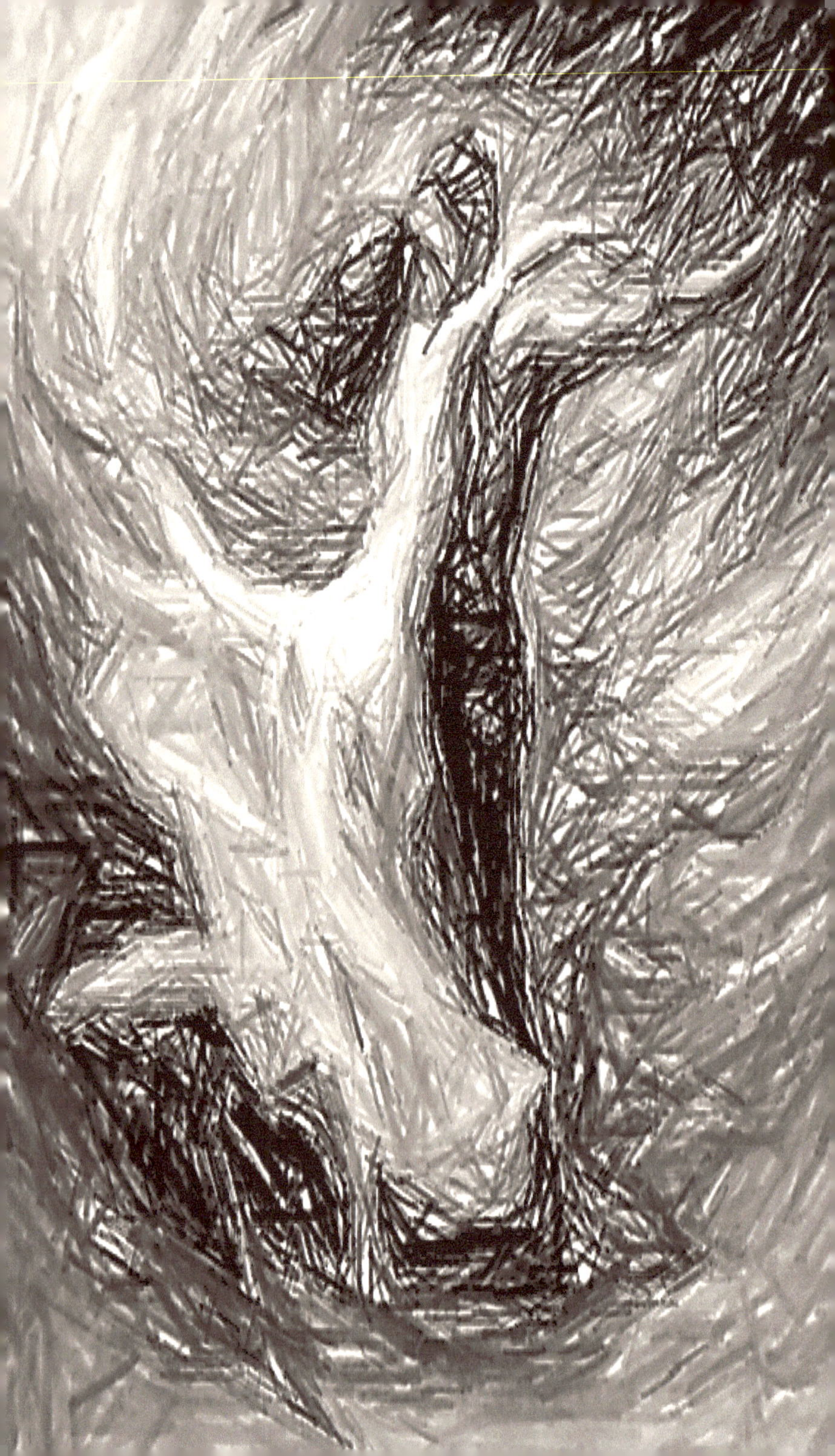

Symphony of Desire

In a crowded room, their souls collide like magnets, pulling
each other toward one another instinctively.
The spark ignites a tempest, converting the chance of whispers
into a beautiful desire.

Each touch ripples across their skin, a reminder of their
intimacy.

Eyes locked as they transcend the ordinary,
silence envelopes them, but it is the language
that is more profound than words.
They are a story waiting to be written —
breathtaking, and timeless.

Where the World Melts

She rests her head on his shoulder and in that simple gesture, the world melts away. In every heartbeat, they find their truths, each pulse echoing the longing in their souls. As they gaze into each other's eyes, the fire burns bright against the shadows. Together they explore every crevice, unearthing their desires, unafraid of what lies beneath. A beautiful chaos, an exquisite dance where love leads every step. In their love, they rediscover themselves, forever twined.

They navigate through laughter and longing, unearthing depths that are previously unknown. Together they redefine a wild dance between fire and gentleness. Each kiss ignites unquenchable flames, radiating warmth that sees through the cold. With each breath, they create a universe filled with hope, where every moment is cherished.

Love as Stardust

The weight of their love is tangible, an embrace that cradles their fears and dreams alike. Each shared moment sparkles like fantasy, with infinite possibility. Each kiss, leaving trails of warmth on their skin.

In the darkness, their hearts converse, speaking volumes only they can see and feel.

Their love is a blazing comet, streaking through the dim sky. With every lingering gaze, they unearth hidden desires, both thrilling and sacred. They are the explorers in uncharted territory, mapping the deep caverns of each other's souls.

And then she wakes up, only to realize, it's just her and the love is just a stardust.

Rhythm of Heart

In the quiet dance of glancing eyes,
Lies the unspoken rhythm, where true love lies.
Hearts whisper softly, words left unsaid,
In the silence, where emotions spread.

Moonlit secrets cast in shadows slight,
Stars bear witness to this gentle plight.
A tender brush of fingertips, unseen,
In the space between breaths, where souls convene.

Whispers Everywhere

There is a delicate, ineffable bond that exists between souls, the ballet of unspoken romance. Conversations woven in silence, a language all their own, communicate what words dare not. Eyes that linger a moment too long, a soft smile exchanged in the hush of a shared secret or the warmth of presence that conveys what neither mouth nor ear can articulate.

It's a romance orchestrated by time's tender hand—a connection that transcends the unspoken word. In the space where words fall short, and actions that whisper promise for love to unfold. These are the moments where feelings flourish, nourished by the quiet understanding and the gentle cadence of shared existence.

This unspoken affection resides in the places where imagination meets reality, in the stolen glimpses and meaningful pauses. A subtle music plays in the background of life's noise, suggesting that sometimes, the deepest connections require no words at all.

Love for Books

Sparkling Dinner

Bella,

my dear,

do you really think loving a vampire is worth all the drama?
Bloodsucking boyfriends come with a lot of baggage—like
constantly avoiding the sunlight or making every dinner date
a midnight affair.

I mean, a romantic dinner under the stars sounds lovely, but
how about we skip the part where you sparkle awkwardly?

Fictional Love

Oh, Mr. Darcy, you are grumpy, brooding lad with your perfectly tailored waistcoat and far too serious demeanor.

Surely, it's not your estate that has me swooning but your ability to brood while tiptoeing around my heart.

Do tell me, when will you learn that sighing dramatically in the rain and flexing your hand is not a substitute for a proper night out?

Obsession

A Hollow Ache

Your absence crafts a hollow ache,
a huge empty cave in my soul, where your laughter once
danced like fireflies in the summer night. Every shared secret
and promise now feels like a cruel joke, a reminder of our
love that slipped through fingers like sand. In the quiet days,
I've learnt to embrace the void and loss. I'm ready to accept
the bittersweet if it means to have truly loved.

Wade Through Shadows

In the stillness of night, I hear your laughter echoing in my memories, a melody that now pierces the silence like a distant star.

Lingering Ghost

I search for your essence in familiar places Only to find the
ghost of moments that can never be reclaimed.

My dear friend, losing you has taught me the weight of
absence, a lesson etched in my soul,
whispering that love, once vibrant, transforms into an ache
that lingers forever.

Lost Love

Sister's Melody

The world feels dimmer without you, sister; your laughter, once a melody, at least that what I remember people saying about you.

I search the skies for your spirit, wishing I could grasp the light you brought, but all I find are stars that twinkle with the weight of our unshared moments.

How unfortunate one could be to not remember the love you showered or should I say, how cruel the world is to take you away from me only to leave a haunting whisper in the silence.

Golden Shadow

At the tender age of two, time unfolded in vibrant hues, a kaleidoscope of childhood moments illuminated by my sister's laughter. She was a shining star in our universe, her presence a warm embrace. In those innocent days, we were unaware of the looming shadow that would steal the brightness away.

Jaundice arrived quietly, a thief cloaked in yellow tones, dimming the sparkle in her eyes. I tried to recall the way she looked, her skin which might have dipped in golden light, a stark contrast to the joy that used to radiate from her smile, I used to remember my mom and my relatives talking about her. Days turned into nights, filled with whispers of caregivers and hushed tones—a language of worry I couldn't yet comprehend the pain. I don't remember any of it. I would trade anything just to remember those days, so that I can tell my son, what a joy of light her aunt was.

The world spun on, indifferent to my little heart breaking, now I know that's how I must have felt, I was just two, who was unaware of the bond that would soon feel like fragile glass. In a matter of moments, she had slipped through our life, leaving behind a silence that echoed louder than any words could express.

Now, almost three decades have crawled by and yet the
weight of loss remains, I have learned to carry her memory
from the stories I heard about her, like a cherished secret.
She is in the flutter of leaves, in the warmth of the sun, in the
laughter of children with curly hair. Each milestone I reach
feels incomplete without her, a reminder of the sister who
once danced through my life.

I often find solace in the belief that love transcends time and space. At 30, I reflect on our moments—the games we might have played, the dreams we might have shared—and while my childhood may have been shadowed, it was also filled with her light. In that truth, I find comfort; she remains as my guiding star in a world where time moves relentlessly forward, yet the bond we shared is an eternal.

Self Love

Today is a Celebration

I pause to soak in the present,
acknowledging my existence
as a beautiful gift.

In the bustling noise of the world,
I find comfort in my own heartbeat
as a reminder of my strength.
While embracing my flaws and
celebrating my strengths,
I transform each doubt
into an act of courage.

In this moment of self-love,
I reclaim my narrative
by writing my story with
intention and
grace.

Lullabies of Silences

In the quiet hours, when the world is asleep, I find myself dancing with the shadows of loneliness and pain. The lullabies of yesterday echo gently while the tender weight of new life rests upon me. I am both cradled and cradler, swaying gently in the symphony of eternity.

The haze of motherhood, a fog that fills the spaces between sleep and wake, wraps around me, blurring the edges of reality. But within this fog, fragments of a world emerge I once knew—a world where laughter rang freely, and time flowed unrestrained.

Here, within this hushed world, I paint pictures with words, where love's gentle tendrils reach across time and space. I found myself writing during every light of dawn, breaking the silence that was too loud for my ears and heart.

With each pen stroke, it felt like a melody, distinct and familiar, binding together the rhythms of my heart. I found myself shaping my narrative anew, finding balance in the shadows and light.

Unrequited Love

Timeless Love

And so, as they walk hand in hand,
hearts beating in Rhythm,
they understand that love is both a journey and destination
—a soft place to land,
also, a hard and rigid place
where a celebration of two souls
can be felt like discovering the beauty
in each other.

Time may flow like an invisible ink,
but in their hearts,
they know their love will always blossom,
a timeless garden cherished by
the simplest truths of life.

Selfish Love

In the Absence of Empathy

In a world that spins on empathy and connection, there exist men who, shrouded in a veil of self-importance, tread the path of selfish love. These men, whose hearts have forgotten the gentle art of empathy, find themselves enthralled by the desires that chant their names in solitude. To them, love is not the nurturing river that flows between souls but a vessel, brimming only for their thirsty ambition.

In relationships painted by selfish love, the nuance of another's heartbeats often fades into silence. Such men, not inherently cold, navigate love as a territory to possess and conquer. Their affection, though fervent, is tethered to the axis of ego, rotating around desires and whims that beckon fulfillment with a magnetic insistence. Within their grasp, love becomes transactional, a ledger where affection is bartered for attention, yet never truly given away.

Every glance, every gesture, is meticulously calculated—not with affection's arithmetic but with a budgeter's scrupulous scrutiny. Time, attention, accolades, they dispense these like measly coins from an otherwise overflowing vault. Here, love becomes a transaction, where the currency is control and the price is another's well-being. What drives this behavior is not simply a lack of feeling, but a fundamental disconnects from the vibration of mutual compassion and understanding.

In dialogues, words flow but intentions snag in the undertow
of control. There lies a strategic calculation rather than
a dance of shared vulnerabilities. Empathy, a language
foreign to selfish love, is hardly spoken, leaving gaps where
understanding should live. Here, the needs of the other
are items on a checklist to occasionally be ticked, rather
than tender whispers exchanged in the quiet of mutual
appreciation.

Yet, beneath the rough exterior often lies a yearning for
connection, even though tangled in the web of self-interest.
It is a dance of shadows - love that insists upon itself,
demanding the script be followed within rigid confines.
But love, to truly flourish, needs liberation; it should be a
symphony of shared echoes, not a solo performance.

In the absence of empathy, space for growth narrows.
Relationships born under selfish love might endure, but not
without a measure of conflict or an aching void of unspoken
longing. Often, the other partner, feeling orphaned of
respect and acknowledgment, treads a path of internalized
disenchantment.

Transformation of this love demands an awakening, one where the men shed their armor of indifference to embrace vulnerability. It is in the unraveling of one's own story, in the acknowledgment of another's journey, that empathy can knit the tapestry anew. Through understanding and open communication, love shifts its form from a selfish possession to a shared odyssey.

In the end, to transcend selfish love is to embrace the chorus of dual harmony, where every note speaks both 'I' and 'we'. It is a reminder that true love, freed from the binds of selfishness, blooms into an expanse where empathy bridges hearts and respect builds foundations - a realm where love truly thrives.

Friend Zoned

i my Love!
BONDING
LAPP
IS (XC)
SNACKEL

Silly Sitcoms

We're speaking different languages—you throw signals, I chuckle at jokes! Let's clear the air: my love language is snack-based bonding. Let's keep the giggles rolling and forget those romantic fables, I love our sitcom of silliness!

The Exclusive Club

You envision romance, but I'm just collecting funny memes. Let's roar with laughter instead of awkward silence; that's the ultimate thrill ride! Let's bask in goofiness, our friendship wrapping around us like the softest blanket. The mismatched pair of giggles unfolds, each moment's like, "Hey, friend, remember that time?"

You took a leap, but my heart's a squirrel—distracted by shiny things! So when you chase romance, I'm over here playing fetch with the puppy of fun with the knowing distracted heart!

Your hopeful heart collides with my laughter, and there's only room for the burst of silliness!

Infatuation

Fleeting Glance

She feels him too, an undeniable pull, as if gravity itself has shifted to draw them together. His eyes, a deep ocean, hold stories untold, depths she yearns to explore. With each fleeting glance, a spark ignites, illuminating the spaces between them, filling silent words.

The brush of hands as they reach for the same book, a shared smile across a crowded room.

Longing and Yearning

Scattered Petals

I trace your outline in the air while I see my fingers tremble at the thought of letting go. I collect your whispers like scattered petals, pressing them between pages, just to get the imprint before it withers completely, my only joy, of what was never truly mine.

Longing for the Unreturned

I write you letters, penned in invisible ink, full of confessions
I will never send, even when I know that it was written to an
affection that's unreturned.
Though the world spins on, I remain rooted in this moment,
forever caught between friendship and longing.
I sketch our moments on the canvas of my mind, with the
vivid landscapes of laughter and light, but they fade like old
photographs, untouched by time. But my dear friend, my
heart always wanders were we left, so if you ever felt the
need to revisit, remember, each flower you see here holds the
memory of what I cannot hold.

A Sweet Ache

In the quiet corners of my heart, a spark ignites, dancing like fireflies in the dusk. Each glance shared sends ripples through my thoughts, a gentle breeze pulling me closer to the warmth of your smile.

In crowded spaces, my eyes find only you, a beacon of light amidst shadows, igniting a yearning that consumes me whole.

Time bends and stretches in your presence, each moment is precious, feels like a glitter in the sun, yet dripping through my fingers like water.

As the night turns into dawn, I am left with the sweet ache of longing, knowing that even the briefest of encounters can leave a lasting mark on the soul.

My Universe –
My Mom

Love Mosaic

In the quiet shadows of our home, my mother became both the sun and the moon, illuminating paths with her unwavering strength. After the separation, when love seemed to disappear like mist, she stood strong, embracing each challenge with the grace of a warrior. Her heart bore the scars of loss, a child taken too soon by the cruel grip of jaundice, a wound that never fully healed but transformed into a reservoir of compassion.

Each day, she put on her armor of determination, facing the echoes of sorrow that haunted our home. The aroma of coffee filled the air, mingling with the sounds of her sewing machine, a lullaby for the echoes of sorrow that lurked in the corners. With every breakfast served, she fed not just our bodies but our spirits, nourishing us with hope and perseverance. Each meal was silent proof to her love, a reminder that she could create beauty even in the face of despair. Her hands, worn yet wise, etched stories into our lives. They taught me to tie my shoelaces, to weave dreams into reality, and to always find joy in the little things—a butterfly's dance, a soft rain, a favorite song playing on repeat. I've never told her that.

In moments of silence, I would catch glimpses of her fragility—lost in thought, a shadow passing over her features as memories flickered like candlelight. Yet, she would shake it off by getting back to the humming of her work. As I grew, so did my understanding of her sacrifices. The late nights spent working, her dreams tucked away in a drawer, waiting for the right moment to breathe again. She wore her determination like a badge, fiercely guarding our happiness. Each sacrifice was a silent vow, a promise that love transcends loss and our family, though reshaped by grief, remains the heart's true endeavor.

In her eyes, I found the courage to forge my path. They sparkled with wisdom, reflecting the trials she had faced. She taught me to rise, to fight, and to embrace life with open arms, even when it felt heavy. As I wandered through the years, her love became my compass, guiding me through life. She was not just my mother but my anchor, my close friend, the embodiment of resilience. In her laughter, I heard the whispers of hope and her tears echoed strength.

My mother, the definition of love, imperfect and whole, a
mosaic of experiences that shaped who I am. Where sorrow
and joy intertwine, I honor her—a mother whose love,
resilient and boundless, transcends time, echoing like a
whispered promise: no matter the struggles, we rise, we love,
and we endure.

Long Distant
Love

A Delicate Dance

In the delicate dance of arranged marriage , I stepped into a path paved by my mother's gentle hands. Through her eyes, I glimpsed a stranger, and he, too, caught the essence of me—a love forged not in the glow of romance but in the warmth of familial intention.

Across the digital world, we exchanged glances wrapped in uncertainty, with my fiancés voice resonating through video calls, both foreign and familiar. Our meeting was a harvest of cautious dreams, each call a fragile thread trying to connect two souls. We ventured into shy laughter and shared hopes, wrapped in silences while trying to build a bridge of understanding.

The days unfolded delicately, as our families met, two worlds converging like rivers flowing toward one another, culminating in our sacred union—a marriage blessed in the rich hues of Brahmin customs. Two days before the wedding—a fleeting moment in time—we finally poured our hearts into each other's gaze, out from the digital window and yet remained as strangers, bound by promises.

Surrounded by fragrant garlands and sacred chants, we
vowed our lives to each other, a week of laughter and shared
dreams that sailed too swiftly, like petals caught in the wind.
But destiny with its intricate plans steered us in unexpected
directions. As he and his family returned to New Zealand,
I found myself waiting—not just for my visa, but for the
promise of our shared tomorrows. Each day was a flicker of
longing while we embraced the stillness with hope.

And the world plunged into a pandemic's grip, the silence of lockdown isolating us for two long years. Time stretched, and our love became a fragile thread connecting only through video calls and messages, a lifeline connecting our heart.

And as we waited, we embraced the beauty of our journey, aware that every moment of separation only strengthened the bond we shared, waiting for the day when we could finally write the next verses of our story together.

The Sand Between Our Toes

Walking along the shore of my memory, I imagine your hand in mine, our footprints mingling in the warm sand. Each grain represents the moments shared and those yet to come, countless and unique like our story. The ocean breeze carries our essence, leaving whispers of intimacy to envelop me as I reminisce. The rhythm of the waves mimics the beat of my heart, crashing with the same intensity I feel for you.

I believe we will walk together again soon, the sand between our toes, reclaiming what distance cannot take away.

Seasons of Waiting

Like the changing seasons, my heart cycles through phases of waiting, yearning for the bloom of our reunion.

Winter stretches its icy fingers, and yet I find warmth in the memories we have talked about crafting together.

Spring brings renewal, brightening my hope with every flower that blossoms, each petal a testament to our love.

Summer's warmth reminds me that soon, the sun will shine upon us together again, casting shadows of what once was.

Autumn arrives, swirling leaves mimic the emotions within me, from joy to melancholy, each breath is a reminder of your absence. The passage of time ebbs and flows, yet love remains constant as the stars that guide me home.

I fill my heart with the promise of your touch, counting the days until I can finally hold you close. Until then, I embrace each season, knowing they are the chapters of our beautiful story waiting to be experienced.

Treasured Memories

A Bond Beyond Blood

He was my first best friend, a partner in all things mischievous—climbing trees to the highest branches, our creativity soaring alongside the birds. When the world felt heavy, he was the gentle breeze that lifted my spirits, the reassuring presence who wiped away tears with a comforting smile.

Every summer afternoon spent beneath the sprawling branches of ancient trees was imbued with our wild imagination, our laughter echoing like music, harmonizing seamlessly while we prepare our magic potions out of lemon leaves.

Whenever confusion brewed within me, he was the windless stream, finding ways to lift my spirits with a wink or a silly joke that turned sorrow into laughter. In those moments, I learned the beauty of unconditional love—the kind that siblings share, a resilient connection that anchors the heart.

He is the keeper of my secrets, the one who hears my heart speak when words and worlds fail.

A cousin who became the sibling , a companion who emerged as my first best friend. Together, we are two souls navigating this world, forever etched in each other's lives, carving a legacy of friendship that time cannot erase.

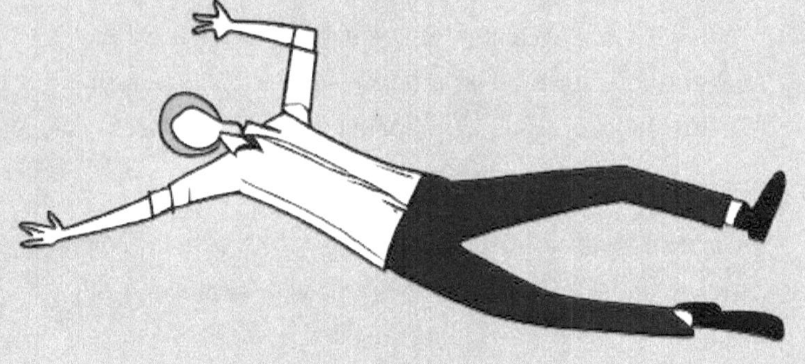

Wheels, Wits and a Sprinkle of Chaos

There was a time when my younger brother and I were masters of the art of skipping language class, seeking refuge in the hallowed halls of the library instead. The promise of thrilling tale was simply too tempting to resist.

On one particular evening , with our imaginations ignited, we hopped on our trusty bicycle, vision boards loaded with fantasies and comical escapades. But, as often happens in epic tales, the universe had different plans.

Our first sign of trouble arrived in the form of a flat tire—the two-wheeled chariot now a sad, deflated mess. "Great, just great!" I sighed, feeling like the hero whose steed had been turned into a pumpkin. To make matters worse, we had discovered, we were five rupees short to fix our mighty steed!

"No problem!" I exclaimed, with the confidence of a
seasoned adventurer. With determination stronger than
a superhero's cape, he, my brother, raced home, eager to
fetch the needed coins, only to face yet another twist of
fate. Caught up in our urgency, experienced an unexpected
encounter with the ground—a small accident that remains
seared in our memories as if etched in stone.

There he was, sprawled out like a dramatic character from a
slapstick comedy, while I stood frozen in a mix of concern and
tears. Two decades later, that moment which now turns into a
hilarious moment, remains vivid. A delightful reminder that
sometimes, the best stories come not from grand encounters,
but from the chaos of brotherly misadventures.

Life,
it seems, has a way of throwing in a little humor with some
literal stones, especially when you least expect it! Embrace it
and love what might come.

Bygone Days

Old memories, old fashioned times, I shall write about my bygone days,

Each evening began with a sense of adventure, as my cousins and I start on our playful journey, armed with our rustic rented bicycles. For just 50 paise, these bicycles were our golden tickets to freedom and delight.

We zigzagged through busy lanes where people carry their washed clothes on their heads, while our tires tracing narratives of innocence. Each tumble became a delightful spectacle, rolling us onto gravel and giggles, our faces etched with dusty smiles. Rising, holding back the tears, we dusted off remnants of play, only to chase each other with renewed vigor.

The air was alive, with the music of our innocence, as we shouted our names. "Catch me if you can!" one would shout, pedaling furiously, while the rest followed, a chorus of names on the wind, binding us closer with every joyful call.

Neighbors, familiar faces etched with warmth, would smile at our antics and some would shout, asking us to slow down, their eyes twinkling with a recognition of simpler joys. They knew us well, their smiles were like blessings, wrapping us in warmth and sense of belonging, silently cheering us on our ride.

Each evening was a lesson in resilience, each chase a chapter
in the book of cherished childhood memories. Our laughter
was the soundtrack to a time where worries were as fleeting
as the passing shower and love was the invisible thread that
bound us together, forever.

While I write this, I tell myself, this is the universe way
of asking me to celebrate the simplicity and purity of our
treasured love.

Love for Foods

When Rice Cakes Twerk

In the bustling heart of the city, where street noise serves as background music, there lies a dish so compelling it could lure anyone with its delicious siren: Tteokbokki!

Each rice cake, plump and proud, floats in that fiery ocean of gochujang sauce, like little edible lifebuoys.

These slick, chewy morsels are basically the food's version of bubble wrap—impossible to resist.

The sauce? It's a spicy tidal wave that crashes over your taste buds with all the subtlety of a marching band in a library. It makes you sweat like you have run a marathon in a sauna.

Taking a bite, my taste buds do a cha-cha-cha with the spiciness, smooth like butter yet it sets my mouth on fire more effectively than an accidental pepper spray incident.

I have a sneaking suspicion that tteokbokki is made from tiny mouthful of happiness—each piece whispering promises of a spicy paradise as you bite down. People say true love is blind, but for me, it is terribly red and deliciously addictive.

It's the spicy hug in a bowl, sweetly suggesting that extra chilly never killed anyone… much.

Here's to tteokbokki, the delightfully dramatic dish that keeps my palate entertained and my mealtimes exciting.

Rock on, spicy rice cake powerhouse!

Friendship

My Dearest Chuckaboo

In the story of my life, you are a pivotal chapter, adding joy and meaning with every beautifully shared moment. Our silly laughter is the song that turns even the cloudy days bright in life's ever-changing weather.

Together, we travel through this world, crafting memories that are cherished and unforgettable. You are my confidant, grounding me when I need it most. Our understanding goes beyond words, each shared experience a bond that deepens our friendship. Only we know even a simplest cheese sandwich date can make our heart flutter.

To my lighthouse, who guides me from a distant, I hope you know this one is for you. True friendship is a rare, gentle love, like a soft melody that plays in the soul's quiet corners. It's the kind of love everyone should embrace, an art of connection that colors our days with profound joy. To have you is a BLISS.

From Rain to Roots

In the intoxicating presence of petrichor, I am wrapped up by a sense of nostalgia and belonging, much like the bond I share with my cousins. They are more than family; they are the cornerstones of my life, my reliable companions who stand by me through every confused noise and tranquility. Every meeting with them is a revival—a gentle storm of shared joys, memories, and love that washes over us, leaving us closer and more connected. They are the first few drops that hint at the rain to come, a promise of connection amid the chaos of life.

With them, words flow as freely as the rain slides down a parched hillside, rejuvenating and vital. Secrets are whispered like the soft patter of raindrops on leaves, each one grounding me, each one a connection to safer place.

Together, they are my constellation of strength and love, a support system that exists beyond mere blood relation. In their presence, I find my anchor. Just as the scent of petrichor lingers, so does the sense of comfort they provide, always drawing me back to our shared roots no matter how far I may roam.

Love for Little Things

In the quiet moments of a morning sun rising, casting rays that dance upon the earthy rooftops of busy city. A pot of milk simmers on the stove, while the coffee brews, filling the air with rich warmth. The dark liquid swirling like dreams awakening in its filter cup.

While the gentle aroma wafts through the air, filling your senses. Each sip is rich and a blend of deep flavors that awaken our mind and body, setting a peaceful tone for the day ahead.

Outside, the call of a temple bell resonates, a melodic announcement to the day, where red hibiscus blooms, sway softly in the breeze. Street vendors begin their morning rituals, the sound of sizzling dosa on a hot tawa, harmonizing with the chatter of early risers.

Children rush to school, their laughter ringing like delicate chimes, while the vibrant colors of their uniforms blend with the world around them, each step a dance of innocence on streets lined with vibrant rangoli patterns.

The warm embrace of a mother's love felt in the way she packs a tiffin, filled with fragrant of lemon rice with potato fry and sweet mango slices, a reminder that home is where the heart, and flavor resides.

As a quiet evening unfolds, the glow of diyas illuminates the night, flickering flames symbolizing hope and togetherness. Family gathers in the living room, sharing stories that weave the past with the present, while laughter dances like fireflies in the darkness. While the taste of bhaji, warm and syrupy, becomes a moment of sweetness held in shared delight, swirling memories around every bite.

With friends, the sight of tantalizing pani puri, bursting with zest, is a celebration of life's flavors—a small joy wrapped in that crispy sphere makes the evening a never ending celebration.

In the heart of it all lies the essence of our life—a symphony of simplicity and richness, where the mundane transforms into the extraordinary. It reminds us to embrace every little moment—a kind word, a shared meal, a festival's light—as sacred, situating us in a world pulsating with life and love and painting our everyday existence with the vivid colors of culture and tradition, to understand that life's richness is woven into the little things—the ones we often overlook, yet they shape our very existence.

Acknowledgements

Writing this book during one of the most transformative times in my life has been both a challenge and a joy. I want to express my heartfelt gratitude to everyone who played a role in this journey.

Firstly, to my mom, Kala, for her unwavering encouragement and continuous support in everything I do. Your belief in me and in my dreams never faltered, even when I doubted myself. You are my world and my entire universe.

Thanks to my brother, who is always there to lift my spirits up when I tumble. Thank you for cheering me on every single new beginning.

To my husband, thank you for your unwavering support and love.

Special thanks and kisses to my son, Vi, whose presence has been my greatest source of inspiration. Your arrival in this world brought a new perspective into my life and writing. You taught me the true meaning of resilience and patience, attributes that have helped complete what I have started.

I'm immensely grateful to my editor and my cheerleader and a friend Aishwarya Kathiravan for your expertise and guidance. Your constructive feedback helped shape this book into its final form and your constant encouragement helped me balance writing with my everyday life.

To my friends, thank you for your understanding and support. Whether it was offering a listening ear or helping with emotional support, your support lightened my load immensely and pulled these words to create a book from my heart.

Finally, thank you to my readers, my insta audience. Your interest in this work during its conception to its final form is deeply appreciated. Knowing that my words will resonate with you keeps me motivated as a new mother and author.

Completing this book while embracing the roles of pregnancy and new motherhood has been a journey like no other. I am forever grateful for the team of incredible family, friends, and professionals who helped me navigate this path.

Author Bio

Harini is an Indian writer who discovered her affinity with verse a few years ago, realising her personal reflections deserved more than just being scribbled on random pages. A former accountant with a knack for numbers, she has traded spreadsheets for lines of metaphor and columns of similes. Harini believes that words can transform emotions into vivid colour and she aims to make the mundane extraordinary: one line at a time. When she's not penning her thoughts, you can find her savouring flavours, getting lost in books or wandering through bookstores. Dive into her lyrical landscape, where every line tells a story!

You can follow Harini on Instagram at @owlyouneedisdrama_books.

As the sun sets on this collection, I leave you with this question: What stories linger in silence, waiting for your voice to bring them to life?